HOW DO PEOPLE PREPARE FOR SEVERE WEATHER?

by Nancy Dickmann

raintree
a Capstone company — publishers for children

Raintree is an imprint of Capstone Global Library Limited, a company incorporated in England and Wales having its registered office at 264 Banbury Road, Oxford, OX2 7DY – Registered company number: 6695582

www.raintree.co.uk
myorders@raintree.co.uk

Text © Capstone Global Library Limited 2022
The moral rights of the proprietor have been asserted.

All rights reserved. No part of this publication may be reproduced in any form or by any means (including photocopying or storing it in any medium by electronic means and whether or not transiently or incidentally to some other use of this publication) without the written permission of the copyright owner, except in accordance with the provisions of the Copyright, Designs and Patents Act 1988 or under the terms of a licence issued by the Copyright Licensing Agency, 5th Floor, Shackleton House, 4 Battle Bridge Lane, London SE1 2HX (www.cla.co.uk). Applications for the copyright owner's written permission should be addressed to the publisher.

Edited by Mandy Robbins
Designed by Heidi Thompson
Original illustrations © Capstone Global Library Limited 2022
Picture research by Tracy Cummins
Production by Katy LaVigne
Originated by Capstone Global Library Ltd
Printed and bound in India

978 1 3982 1517 7 (hardback)
978 1 3982 1518 4 (paperback)

British Library Cataloguing in Publication Data
A full catalogue record for this book is available from the British Library.

Acknowledgements
We would like to thank the following for permission to reproduce photographs: Alamy: Sipa USA/Alamy Live News, 13; Getty Images: Mark Wilson, 19; iStockphoto: Deepak Sethi, 11, SDI Productions, 29; Newscom: REUTERS/Rick Wilking, 23; Shutterstock: Arthur Villator, 18, CGN089, 26, DeSerg, 15, FotoKina, cover, design element, 1, FrameStockFootages, 8, Hryshchyshen Serhii, 17, littlenySTOCK, 16, Makhnach_S, design element, Minerva Studio, 9, Nancy Beijersbergen, 5, Pat Lauzon, 6, Robert Blouin, 28, Roger Brown Photography, 14, Shane Wilson, 7, Steve Allen, 20, Suzanne Tucker, 4, Vadym Zaitsev, 25, wannapong, 21, wavebreakmedia, 27

Every effort has been made to contact copyright holders of material reproduced in this book. Any omissions will be rectified in subsequent printings if notice is given to the publisher.

All the internet addresses (URLs) given in this book were valid at the time of going to press. However, due to the dynamic nature of the internet, some addresses may have changed, or sites may have changed or ceased to exist since publication. While the author and publisher regret any inconvenience this may cause readers, no responsibility for any such changes can be accepted by either the author or the publisher.

CONTENTS

What is severe weather? 4

Having a plan 10

Be prepared! 18

After the storm 28

Glossary 30

Find out more. 31

Index 32

Words in **bold** are in the glossary.

WHAT IS SEVERE WEATHER?

A storm is coming! The weather will be rainy and windy. Weather describes the conditions in the air around us. Weather changes all the time. It can change slowly. Sometimes it changes very quickly.

A thunderstorm is one example of severe weather. It has strong winds and heavy rain. Severe weather can damage buildings. It can hurt people. It also harms plants and animals.

Types of severe weather

Weather usually follows patterns. Severe weather patterns are extreme. The temperature might be very high or low. There may be heavy snowstorms. These are called **blizzards**.

Heavy rain is another type of severe weather. It can lead to **flooding**. Rain often comes as part of a storm. Storms can bring high winds too. **Hurricanes** have very strong winds. So do **tornadoes**.

OTHER STORMS
Storms do not always have wind and rain. In a dust storm, huge clouds of dust blow across the land. Ice storms can coat everything in a layer of ice.

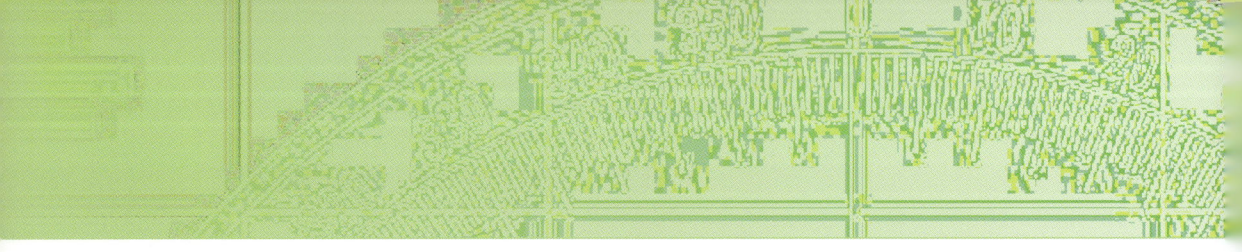

Predicting severe weather

People need to be ready for severe weather. A **forecast** can tell what the weather will be like. It warns if a storm is coming.

Meteorologists study **satellite** images of the weather. They might see a hurricane forming. Where will it go? A computer program will help them to work it out. Tornadoes are harder to **predict**. They can form with little warning.

A tornado touches down.

HAVING A PLAN

Severe weather can strike quickly. Having a plan is important. Businesses, schools and families all make plans for severe weather. Then everyone will know what to do.

Where do you live? Some types of severe weather may be more likely there. Different weather calls for different emergency plans.

An emergency plan will help people stay safe. It can tell people where to go. It will include a list of supplies they may need.

A family creates an emergency plan.

Practice and drills

In weather **drills**, people practise what to do in a storm. Schools in some countries have tornado drills. An alarm sounds. Pupils move quickly to a safe place. They learn what to do in a real tornado.

Some cities have sirens. They sound when severe weather is coming. There are warnings on the radio and TV. Some people get text alerts. The texts say when to go to a safe place.

A teacher supervises a tornado drill at school.

Emergency supplies

When severe weather happens, shops may be closed. Many families have an emergency kit. It is full of supplies. It will be ready if they need it.

A good emergency kit has enough food for a few days. The food should not need to go in the fridge. The kit will have enough bottled water for everyone. It will also include a first-aid kit. A radio is useful too.

A battery-operated radio lets you hear the news even if the power goes off.

Losing power

Sometimes the power goes off in severe weather. There is no **electricity**. Lights will not work. TVs won't work either. This is called a power cut. It might last for an hour. It could last for days or weeks.

Severe weather often causes trees to fall on power lines. This causes power cuts.

A woman uses a torch to read to a child during a power cut.

People may have to go without electricity. An emergency kit should include a torch and batteries. A portable charger uses a battery too. It can charge a mobile phone.

BE PREPARED!

Preparing for hurricanes

Hurricanes have very strong winds. They cause a lot of damage. People listen to the forecast. They may be told to leave their homes before the hurricane hits. They will go to a safer area. They can return when the storm passes.

A storm wave crashes onto a coastal road.

People can prepare their homes. They close **shutters** or put boards over windows. This stops the glass from breaking. If it is safe to stay at home, people stay inside. They stay far away from windows.

Rescue workers save a family from a flooded area.

Preparing for floods

Floods happen when water overflows onto the land. Heavy rain can cause floods. So can hurricanes. Sometimes flood waters rise slowly. At other times floods happen quickly. Floodwater can carry people and cars away. It can cover houses.

Many places can have flood warnings. Sometimes the safest thing to do is leave the area. You can pack a bag and go to a safer place. It is best to leave before the flood hits. It is not safe to drive through floodwaters.

Floodwaters cover cars in a car park.

Preparing for tornadoes

Tornadoes are funnels of wind. The wind is very strong. It can flip cars. It can blow roofs off buildings. It can destroy homes. Tornadoes strike quickly. People need to move fast.

There will be a warning when a tornado is likely. People have to get to a safe place. This could be a basement. It could also be a small room or cupboard with no windows. People use their arms to cover their head and neck.

A family gathers in a bathroom with no windows during a tornado.

PREDICTING TORNADOES

Most tornadoes form in a thunderstorm. They are most likely to happen in spring and summer. Meteorologists track storms. They look for clouds that could form tornadoes. They send out warnings.

Preparing for blizzards

A blizzard is a heavy snowstorm. It will be very cold. Icy winds can blow fast. Several centimetres of snow may fall. It is not safe to drive in a blizzard.

The power may go off. If a house uses electric heat, it may not work. It is important to keep warm. People gather supplies before a blizzard hits. They may be stuck inside for several days. They make sure they have plenty of blankets and warm clothes.

Preparing for a heat wave

Sometimes weather gets very hot and **humid**. It might last for several days. This is called a heat wave. Getting too hot can make people unwell. Some people even die. It's important to stay cool.

Closing the curtains is a good idea. Doing this can stop a building from getting too hot. People should also stay out of the sun. They should drink plenty of water. Sometimes people find a place that has air conditioning. This could be a home, a library or a shopping centre.

AFTER THE STORM

Severe weather doesn't last forever. But there may still be dangers right after it passes. Buildings may be damaged. Power lines might be down. It might not be safe to go out.

Homes may need repairs. People might need to replace their emergency supplies. Everyone can pitch in and help each other. If severe weather strikes again, everyone will be ready!

GLOSSARY

blizzard heavy snowstorm with strong wind; a blizzard can last several days

drill learn something by doing it over and over again

electricity natural force used to make light and heat or to make machines work

flood overflow with water beyond the normal limits

forecast report of future weather conditions

humid damp or moist

hurricane strong, swirling wind and rainstorm that starts on the ocean

meteorologist person who studies and predicts the weather

predict say what you think will happen in the future

satellite spacecraft used to send signals and information from one place to another

shutter hinged panel that can be closed to cover a glass window

tornado violent spinning column of air that makes contact with the ground

FIND OUT MORE

BOOKS

Weather and the Seasons, DK (DK Children, 2019)

Weather: Get Hands-On with Geography (Discover and Do!), Jane Lacey (Franklin Watts, 2021)

What are Blizzards? (Wicked Weather), Mari Schuh (Raintree, 2019)

What are Thunderstorms? (Wicked Weather), Mari Schuh (Raintree, 2019)

WEBSITES

www.bbc.co.uk/bitesize/topics/z849q6f/articles/z7dkhbk
Learn more about weather and climate.

www.dkfindout.com/uk/earth/weather
Find out more about weather.

INDEX

clouds 7, 23

emergency kits 14–15, 17

emergency plans 10

floods 7, 20–21

forecasts 8, 18

heat waves 26–27

meteorologists 9, 23

power cuts 16–17, 24, 28

rain 4, 5, 7, 20

satellites 9

sirens 12

snow 6, 24

storms 4, 7, 8, 12, 18, 23
   blizzards 6, 24
   dust storms 7
   hurricanes 7, 9, 18, 20
   ice storms 7
   thunderstorms 5, 23

temperature 6

tornadoes 7, 9, 12, 22, 23

warnings 9, 12, 21, 22, 23

weather drills 12

wind 4, 5, 7, 18, 22, 24